James

30-DAY DEVOTIONAL

James

Stuart Briscoe
with Elizabeth McQuoid

FOOD
FOR THE
JOURNEY

INTER-VARSITY PRESS
36 Causton Street, London SW1P 4ST, England
Email: ivp@ivpbooks.com
Website: www.ivpbooks.com

First published 2017

British Library Cataloguing-in-Publication Data
A catalogue record for this book is available from the British Library.

ISBN: 978–1–78359–523–5
eBook ISBN: 978–1–78359–524–2

Typeset in Great Britain by CRB Associates, Potterhanworth, Lincolnshire
Printed and bound by CPI Group (UK) Ltd, Croydon, CR0 4YY

Inter-Varsity Press publishes Christian books that are true to the Bible and that communicate the gospel, develop discipleship and strengthen the church for its mission in the world.

IVP originated within the Inter-Varsity Fellowship, now the Universities and Colleges Christian Fellowship, a student movement connecting Christian Unions in universities and colleges throughout Great Britain, and a member movement of the International Fellowship of Evangelical Students. Website: www.uccf.org.uk. That historic association is maintained, and all senior IVP staff and committee members subscribe to the UCCF Basis of Faith.

Preface

Can you guess how many sermons have been preached from the Keswick platform? Almost 6,500!

For over 140 years, the Keswick Convention in the English Lake District has welcomed gifted expositors from all over the world. The convention's archive is a treasure trove of sermons preached on every book of the Bible.

This series is an invitation to mine that treasure. It takes the Bible Reading series given by well-loved Keswick speakers, past and present, and reformats them into daily devotionals. Where necessary, the language has been updated but, on the whole, it is the message you would have heard had you been listening in the tent on Skiddaw Street. Each day of the devotional ends with a newly written section designed to help you apply God's Word to your own life and situation.

Whether you are a convention regular or have never been to Keswick, this Food for the Journey series is a unique opportunity to study the Scriptures with a Bible teacher by your side. Each book is designed to fit in your jacket pocket or handbag so you can read it anywhere – over the breakfast table, on the commute into work or college, while you are waiting in your car, during your lunch break or in bed at night. Wherever life's journey takes you, time in God's Word is vital nourishment for your spiritual journey.

Our prayer is that these devotionals become your daily feast, a precious opportunity to meet with God through his Word. Read, meditate, apply and pray through the Scriptures given for each day, and allow God's truths to take root and transform your life.

If these devotionals whet your appetite for more, there is a 'For further study' section at the end of each book. You can also visit our website at www.keswickministries.org/resources to find the full range of books, study guides, CDs, DVDs and mp3s available. Why not order an audio recording of the Bible Reading series to accompany your daily devotional?

Let the word of Christ dwell in you richly.
(Colossians 3:16, ESV)

Introduction
James

They were fleeing for their lives.

Stephen's martyrdom in Jerusalem signalled a mass exodus as believers fled throughout the Roman Empire.

As leader of the Jerusalem church, what words of encouragement would James write to these persecuted Christians?

Perhaps a little surprisingly, his key message was: faith works. Genuine belief inevitably transforms our speech, suffering, compassion for the poor, humility, prayers, priorities and every other aspect of life. In just five chapters James introduces and briefly touches upon a whole variety of issues that concern these new believers. He doesn't give an exhaustive treatise on suffering or any other topic, but in a simple, forthright style he urges them to live out their faith, knowing that God's grace is sufficient for every trial and there is a value and purpose to their suffering.

James's own life illustrated his message. He grew up with Jesus and naturally was sceptical about his brother's

Messianic claims. But a post-resurrection encounter with Jesus revolutionized his life. He was transformed from a vocal critic into a key leader of the early church and a prime mover in the Jerusalem Council (Acts 15).

His own experience of transformation and seeing God's grace at work in tandem with personal obedience convinced James that true faith was demonstrated by deeds. There is no such thing as faith without works. The dichotomy doesn't exist – it is not either-or, but both-and. Not that any of these works justify us before God, but they are evidence that we have been justified; that the Holy Spirit is changing us; that sanctification is under way.

Today, in our increasingly secular and materialistic world, as we face a growing tide of pressure to privatize our faith, James's message is still on target. The world is not looking for cheerful triumphalism, statements of belief or empty promises. What the world desperately needs to see is genuine faith demonstrated in the suffering, chaos and unpredictability of everyday life. It needs to witness the transformation that the Holy Spirit makes possible when we yield and are obedient to him.

What do people see when they look at your life?

Do they see faith that works?

Day 1

Read James 1:1–4

Key verses: James 1:1–2

• •

> [1] *James, a servant of God and of the Lord Jesus Christ,*
> *To the twelve tribes scattered among the nations:*
> *Greetings.*
> [2] *Consider it pure joy, my brothers and sisters,*
> *whenever you face trials of many kinds.*

Think back to when you became a Christian. What did you expect? How did you anticipate your life unfolding? Did the preacher promise you blue skies, bright sunshine and a wonderful life?

Jesus challenges this type of thinking when he says to his disciples, 'In this world you will have trouble' (John 16:33). And without any preamble or introduction, James picks up this theme at the start of his letter. He wants his readers to know that trials are inevitable. James does not say, 'Consider it pure joy, my brothers, *if* you face trials.' There is absolutely no question about it; Christians *will* face trials.

James knew that trials were inevitable because:

- He had watched his half-brother, Jesus, suffering intensely.

- He knew the twelve tribes were scattered among the nations.

  In verse 1 James could have been thinking primarily about Jewish history: their captivity under the Assyrians and Babylonians and then dispersion under the Romans. James was well aware that the Jews had been scattered from their homeland all over the world. But it is also possible that he was thinking of the dispersion of the early church. After Stephen was martyred, Christians scattered, fleeing the persecution in Jerusalem. We can't say conclusively to whom he is writing, but the point is that seeing the scattering of believers and the Jews, James was well aware that trials were inevitable.

- He himself had suffered.

  In verse 1 James calls himself 'a servant of God and of the Lord Jesus Christ'. It is true that he was a pillar of the church in Jerusalem (Galatians 2:9) and he chaired the Council at Jerusalem (Acts 15), but nevertheless he calls himself a 'servant'. Servants give of themselves without any regard for their own well-being and do not have any rights to their own life. As James knew, this is a very testing experience because it militates against everything that is inherently human.

James is a church leader who has gone through times of deep testing. Writing from his own wealth of experience, he encourages the scattered and suffering believers to stand firm.

'If God really loved me, he wouldn't let this happen.' Have you ever said or thought that? Have trials caught you off guard, rocked your faith and made you question all you believe about God?

You are not alone.

Most believers have experienced similar thoughts. But God never said that our lives would be any different from those around us or that we would escape suffering. He never suggested that serving him would guarantee us a smooth passage to heaven. Quite the opposite in fact!

Yes, some trials are of our own making because we made wrong choices and have to live with the consequences. But even if we live for God wholeheartedly, trials are inevitable and unavoidable. Don't let them unsettle you (1 Thessalonians 3:2–4). Don't let them throw you off course on your journey of faith. Instead, meditate on God's truth:

> I consider that our present sufferings are not worth comparing with the glory that will be revealed in us . . . For I am convinced that neither death nor life, neither angels nor demons, neither the present nor the future, nor any powers, neither height nor depth, nor anything else in all creation, will be able to separate us from the love of God that is in Christ Jesus our Lord.
> (Romans 8:18, 38)

Day 2

Read James 1:1–4
Key verse: James 1:2

....

> *2Consider it pure joy, my brothers and sisters, whenever you face trials of many kinds.*

If we knew trials were coming, most of us would do our best to avoid them. But that's the trouble: trials usually come suddenly, without any warning.

On a visit to the Philippines I saw an open manhole, and was told it was extremely dangerous during the rain and floods – sometimes people forgot it was there under the water and fell into it. The word James uses for trials conveys the same kind of image: you encounter them unexpectedly.

The same word is used in the story of the Good Samaritan about a certain man going down from Jerusalem who 'fell among robbers' (Luke 10:30, ESV). You remember also that Paul and his companions were sailing in a storm. The ship was falling apart, and then they 'struck a sand-bar' (Acts 27:41). It's exactly the same word.

You fall into a flooded manhole, you fall into the hands of robbers on the way from Jerusalem or you hit a sandbank, and before you know it, you are in over your head. This is the image that James uses to describe how these testing times will come.

And these testings come in many forms. The word James uses is often best translated 'many-coloured', 'variegated'. Christian psychologist Jay Adams puts it this way: 'Our testings can come in the fiery reds of affliction, the icy blues of sorrow, the murky browns of failure, the sickly yellows of illness and disease.'

But just as testing times come in various forms, so does God's grace. Peter, writing on a similar subject, points out that the grace of God comes in variegated forms, using that same word (1 Peter 4:10).

It may not feel like this right now, but whatever your situation, the grace of God is adequate for it.

Bring to God your many-coloured afflictions. Imagine him covering over each one with the rainbow colours of his grace. Allow his grace to equip and restore you and be reflected through you:

'My grace is sufficient for you, for my power is made perfect in weakness.' Therefore I will boast all the more gladly about my weaknesses, so that Christ's power may rest on me.

(2 Corinthians 12:9)

Be strong in the grace that is in Christ Jesus.

(2 Timothy 2:1)

Let us then approach God's throne of grace with confidence, so that we may receive mercy and find grace to help us in our time of need.

(Hebrews 4:16)

And the God of all grace, who called you to his eternal glory in Christ, after you have suffered a little while, will himself restore you and make you strong, firm and steadfast.

(1 Peter 5:10)

Day 3

Read James 1:1–4
Key verses: James 1:3–4

....

> [3] *You know that the testing of your faith produces perseverance.* [4] *Let perseverance finish its work so that you may be mature and complete, not lacking anything.*

When you're suffering, there is nothing more annoying than someone casually telling you to 'Smile! It could be worse.'

James isn't telling us just to cheer up. He says, 'Consider it joy', because trials are valuable and they have a purpose.

Trials test the centre of our faith. We all have faith. The big question is: faith in what? You can have tremendous faith in your own physical fitness until you get sick. You can have tremendous faith in your doctor until he tells you he can't diagnose your problem. The whole point is that faith should be centred on God, who is worthy of our faith. And sometimes it takes testings – trials – to prove to us that the centre of our faith is not where it should be.

Trials are also valuable because they produce perseverance. This does not mean a fatalistic resignation to the inevitable. If we respond appropriately, these testings will produce in us a rugged, patient steadfastness.

And when this spiritual perseverance has been produced, it becomes productive in and of itself. As James explains, 'Let perseverance finish its work so that you may be mature and complete, not lacking anything' (verse 4). The word James uses for 'mature' conveys the idea of attaining the goal, reaching the end point. And the word for 'complete' speaks of a sense of wholeness. In other words, God has a goal in mind for you: being completely like Christ.

And as you trust God and persevere through testing times, the result will be that, slowly but surely, you become more and more like Christ. You will become the person God designed you to be – 'conformed to the image of his Son' (Romans 8:29).

It seems counterintuitive, but trials are valuable and purposeful. They come so that we might not be 'lacking anything'.

Consider the trials you are going through. Why do you think God has permitted them? What lessons does he want to teach you? Are these trials:

- making sure your faith is centred on God?
- purifying your faith?
- developing steadfastness in you?

Don't waste your suffering. Ask God to give you his perspective. Pray that you would be able to see these trials as a gift to make you into the person God designed you to be.

> Consider it a sheer gift, friends, when tests and challenges come at you from all sides. You know that under pressure, your faith-life is forced into the open and shows its true colours. So don't try to get out of anything prematurely. Let it do its work so you become mature and well-developed, not deficient in any way.
>
> (James 1:2–4 MSG)

Day 4

Read James 1:2–11
Key verses: James 1:5–8

....

> [5] *If any of you lacks wisdom, you should ask God, who gives generously to all without finding fault, and it will be given to you.* [6] *But when you ask, you must believe and not doubt, because the one who doubts is like a wave of the sea, blown and tossed by the wind.* [7] *That person should not expect to receive anything from the Lord.* [8] *Such a person is double-minded and unstable in all they do.*

How are you coping with your present trials and testing?

James gives us pointers for how to manage. He encourages us to:

• carefully consider

  Verse 2 begins, 'Consider'. It means to 'count' or 'direct your thinking'. The way you think about a situation will largely determine how you respond to it. And so it is imperative that we get our thinking straight.

- continually confess

We have to confess our lack of wisdom (verse 5). Wisdom is different from knowledge. Knowledge is possessing data, but wisdom is knowing what to do with it. When we talk of lacking wisdom in trials and testing, what we are really saying is: 'What is the right thing to do in response to this situation? And how do I do it?'

As verse 5 reminds us, we have to confess that we need help and ask God for it. We don't just have to roll up our sleeves, grit our teeth and make the best of it; we can ask God for help. We ask in faith, recognizing that we are totally dependent on him for the power to cope with the testing so that the desired end might be achieved – we don't want to be 'double-minded' or 'unstable'.

- cheerfully celebrate

Verse 2 is not telling us to celebrate the tests, but rather to say, 'Today I have a rainbow of varied, many-coloured tests. But I'm glad that you are a generous and gracious God. I know that you have an end in view and I'm glad that these tests give me a chance to identify the centre, core and calibre of my faith. I believe that there's a high probability that if I respond to the wisdom you give me, I'm going to come out of this trial tested and tried like pure gold.'

How are you managing your trials? Are you burying your head in the sand and pretending they're not happening? Are they making you bitter and disillusioned with God? Are you looking around and wondering why other people's lives seem so trial-free? Are you putting on a smile and false triumphalism, waiting for a rose-tinted, pain-free future?

It might be hard, but today will you:

• face your trials head on and acknowledge them for what they are?

> See, I have refined you, though not as silver;
>> I have tested you in the furnace of affliction.
> (Isaiah 48:10)

• confess your need for God's wisdom and strength?

> My God will meet all your needs according to the riches
> of his glory in Christ Jesus.
> (Philippians 4:19)

• celebrate what God is doing in and through you?

> In all this you greatly rejoice, though now for a little while you may have had to suffer grief in all kinds of trials. These have come so that the proven genuineness of your faith – of greater worth than gold, which perishes even though refined by fire – may result in praise, glory and honour when Jesus Christ is revealed. (1 Peter 1:6–7)

Day 5

Read James 1:12–18
Key verses: James 1:13–15, 17–18

. . . .

[13] When tempted, no one should say, 'God is tempting me.' For God cannot be tempted by evil, nor does he tempt anyone; [14] but each person is tempted when they are dragged away by their own evil desire and enticed. [15] Then, after desire has conceived, it gives birth to sin; and sin, when it is full-grown, gives birth to death . . .

[17] Every good and perfect gift is from above, coming down from the Father of the heavenly lights, who does not change like shifting shadows. [18] He chose to give us birth through the word of truth, that we might be a kind of firstfruits of all he created.

'God is tempting me'; 'It's God's fault'; 'The devil made me do it.' We use many creative excuses to rationalize our sin!

Each of us has a whole catalogue of 'desires'. Many of these desires are perfectly legitimate, but they can be twisted, warped and abused. If that happens and we are exposed to external testing, it is possible to be dragged into sin (verse 14). The idea is similar to hooking a fish and dragging it out of the water.

So imagine, for example, a situation comes along and it's not my fault. There is a desire within me that at first was legitimate, but now it has become warped and twisted and I've hung around long enough so the hook is set in my mouth. Before I realize what is happening, I'm being dragged away, and the situation that was a testing to prove me has turned into a temptation that has produced sin and death.

That is how temptation works.

In contrast, there is nothing in God that would respond to an external event in such a way that it could produce sin. He does not tempt. He permits, he ordains, he allows, he uses tempting, but never with a view to our sinning, always with a view to our maturing. And just as the sun, moon and stars go on shining, so he goes on graciously, generously giving to us, unchanging, pure and holy in his character, making available to us all we need, in order that we might respond as we ought. Indeed, God took the divine initiative to give us his Holy Spirit and generate within us a response that would result in new birth. The whole point of this new birth is that we might become mature, holy, a kind of first-fruits to God, the beginning of the harvest.

Have you tasted the metal in your mouth? Your desires have been warped; wrong thinking about yourself and God have made you vulnerable to being dragged into sin. All of a sudden, without realizing it, the devil has you hooked like a fish.

Ask for God's forgiveness today.
Ask for foresight to recognize when you are being tested.
Ask for God's strength not to fall into temptation.
Ask for God's help to use difficult times as a means of maturity and spiritual growth.

Personalize Paul's prayer and make it your own:

We continually ask God to fill you with the knowledge of his will through all the wisdom and understanding that the Spirit gives, so that you may live a life worthy of the Lord and please him in every way: bearing fruit in every good work, growing in the knowledge of God, being strengthened with all power according to his glorious might so that you may have great endurance and patience, and giving joyful thanks to the Father, who has qualified you to share in the inheritance of his holy people in the kingdom of light. For he has rescued us from the dominion of darkness and brought us into the kingdom of the Son he loves, in whom we have redemption, the forgiveness of sins.

(Colossians 1:9–14)

Day 6

Read James 1:19–27
Key verses: James 1:19–20

∙∙∙

> *19 My dear brothers and sisters, take note of this: everyone should be quick to listen, slow to speak and slow to become angry, 20 because human anger does not produce the righteousness that God desires.*

Mark Twain allegedly said, 'It ain't the parts of the Bible I don't understand that bother me, it's the parts I do understand.'

Some parts of the Bible may be opaque and provoke endless discussion and conjecture. But this last section in James 1 couldn't be any clearer. Here he lists, without much comment, God's requirements of us.

These are the things God wants us to do:

• Deal with our anger.

• Deal with our moral filth.

- Do what God's Word says.

- Keep a tight rein on our tongue.

- Help the needy people around us.

The objective behind all these things is to cultivate within us the righteous life that God desires (verse 20). If we do them in the power of the Spirit, drawing on the generous, gracious, ungrudging provision of our God, then when we go through trials, they will not degenerate into temptations, and we will become increasingly mature: the first-fruits – set apart for God.

Read through verses 19–27 again slowly.

Then divide the passage into sections – verses 19–20, 21, 22–25, 26, 27 – and meditate on each topic.

Put these challenges into your own context and situation. Pray through how you can be obedient to God's demands. This isn't about trying harder in your own strength, but rather relying on God's power and wisdom to grow in the midst of trials. God's aim is our spiritual transformation: that we become all that he designed us to be, or as the Danish philosopher Søren Kierkegaard prayed, 'And now Lord, with your help, I shall become myself.'

Day 7

Read James 2:1–4
Key verse: James 2:1

....

¹My brothers and sisters, believers in our glorious Lord Jesus Christ must not show favouritism.

Are you judicious and courteous when you are trying to make your point, or are you direct and forthright? We each have our own individual style!

James's style is usually blunt and straight to the point.

He is eager to remind his readers that their religion is to be characterized by a marked concern for the under-privileged. He introduced this theme in 1:27: 'Religion that God our Father accepts as pure and faultless is this: to look after orphans and widows in their distress.' His concern is that practical spiritual experience should manifest itself in compassion for orphans, widows and the impoverished.

However, there is warmth to his plea. He addresses it to 'my brothers and sisters', those who, because they have been born of the same Spirit, born through the same engrafted Word, are members of the same family. He is speaking to his fellow believers: literally, 'those who hold the faith'.

The reason why we are not to show favouritism is because of 'our glorious Lord Jesus Christ'. He is our standard, the One we look to, our model. And Jesus didn't show favouritism because his Father didn't. Remember that God strictly instructed the Levites: 'Do not pervert justice; do not show partiality to the poor or favouritism to the great, but judge your neighbour fairly' (Leviticus 19:15). Or think back to Peter's vision as he slept on the rooftop of Simon the tanner's house. His vision of the unclean foods taught him that God did not discriminate between Jews and Gentiles, and when he got to Cornelius's house, he declared, 'I now realise how true it is that God does not show favouritism' (Acts 10:34). God's lack of favouritism is not an isolated theme; it runs throughout Scripture (see Romans 2:11; Ephesians 6:9; Colossians 3:25; 1 Timothy 5:21).

The very title, 'Lord Jesus Christ', reminds us that he is Lord of all, not just some; he is Jesus the Saviour, who died for all, not just some; he is the Christ, the Anointed One, the sent One, who came for all, not just some.

The glory of the Lord Jesus insists that we model ourselves on him and do not show favouritism.

Who are you modelling your faith on? Sometimes our role models are church leaders. Their public display of Christianity informs how we behave and what we prioritize. Often, without intending to, we make our Christian friends our role models. We let their spirituality set the temperature for ours; their passion for Christ and level of discipleship dictate ours.

James challenges us not to let other believers set the pace for our devotion to God. Our only model must be the 'glorious Lord Jesus Christ'. He longs for us to model Christ in our:

- prayer life
- faithful service
- compassion for the sick and marginalized
- humility
- obedience to God
- perseverance and patience during trials
- passion to share the gospel.

Pray through all the aspects of your day. Ask for the Holy Spirit's help to model Jesus everywhere you go, in everything you do – in all your conversations and decisions, your thoughts and attitudes, at work and in your leisure time.

Day 8

Read James 2:1–4
Key verses: James 2:2–4

....

[2] Suppose a man comes into your meeting wearing a gold ring and fine clothes, and a poor man in filthy old clothes also comes in. [3] If you show special attention to the man wearing fine clothes and say, 'Here's a good seat for you,' but say to the poor man, 'You stand there' or 'Sit on the floor by my feet,' [4] have you not discriminated among yourselves and become judges with evil thoughts?

Have you ever looked at some politician, celebrity or athlete and thought, 'Wouldn't that person make a wonderful Christian?' Why? Because it would be wonderful for *us* if he or she was a Christian! It would help our finances, status and credibility.

That is just one example of favouritism. In these verses James gives his readers another. He describes the poor people in this impoverished church evaluating a newcomer according to external criteria. They reason that because he is wearing fine clothes and a gold ring, he must be a man of substance, and because he is a man of substance, he must be deserving of special treatment.

At the same time a poor man comes in, in filthy old clothes. The congregation wonder where they can park him! The decision is made: 'Go and stand over there in the corner', or 'There's a seat here at my footstool.' If there was one thing that insulted a Jew more than anything else, it was telling that person to sit down at somebody's feet. It was like saying, 'Lick my boots!'

James's example probably isn't hypothetical. We know that the church in Jerusalem, where he was a prominent leader, was very poor. Remember that the apostle Paul spent a considerable amount of time raising money to go to the aid of this Jerusalem church. So if a very poor church was suddenly visited by an ostentatiously wealthy man, what a temptation it would be to put on a show for him.

James's point is that these Christians are evaluating by externals. They are quick to act in prejudice. And they are opportunistic; doubtless they can see advantages in befriending a wealthy newcomer. James wants them to see that they are discriminating among themselves, they are coming to judgmental positions about people and this is evil thinking!

Think through your own propensity for favouritism:

- At the end of the church service, do you tend to make a beeline for your friends, or do you look out for those who need encouragement and a listening ear?
- Do you look for ways to ingratiate yourself with the 'influencers' in your church?
- Think about the Christians you invite round for meals or meet up with during the week – are they mainly people in your social bracket, those with children the same age as yours?

To gauge whether favouritism is operating in your church, consider how newcomers feel. Do they receive a warm welcome on a Sunday and at the various mid-week groups? Or would they notice that you have to act, dress and worship a certain way in order to be accepted?

Paul reminds us that natural affiliations have no place in how we are to treat one another. We are all children of God and blood-bought brothers and sisters in Christ. Meditate on Galatians 3:26–29. Ask God to show you any favouritism you need to tackle and evil thinking you need to correct.

So in Christ Jesus you are all children of God through faith, for all of you who were baptised into Christ have clothed yourselves with Christ. There is neither Jew nor Gentile, neither slave nor free, nor is there male and female, for you are all one in Christ Jesus. If you belong to Christ, then you are Abraham's seed, and heirs according to the promise.

(Galatians 3:26–29)

Day 9

Read James 2:5–10
Key verses: James 2:5–7

. . . .

⁵Listen, my dear brothers and sisters: has not God chosen those who are poor in the eyes of the world to be rich in faith and to inherit the kingdom he promised those who love him? ⁶But you have dishonoured the poor. Is it not the rich who are exploiting you? Are they not the ones who are dragging you into court? ⁷Are they not the ones who are blaspheming the noble name of him to whom you belong?

Have you 'dishonoured the poor'?

This may seem rather an extreme statement. Perhaps you feel you have not 'dishonoured the poor' as much as not thought about them. Except, of course, when you see someone selling *The Big Issue* in the shopping centre.

For many of us, God's care for the poor stands in sharp contrast to our own.

Far from overlooking the poor, God often chooses them to be rich in faith (verse 5). Amazingly, God chooses, enriches and uses the most unlikely people. He has a delightful way of doing things exactly the opposite way we would do them. So if we look at people simply on the basis of their external appearance, we might miss somebody who under their shabby clothing is actually rich in faith – a wonderful believer, a member of the kingdom, somebody who really loves the Lord.

You are making a wrong choice if you side with the rich rather than the poor. These people insult those whom God honours, exploit the poor and drag you into court (verse 6). James may have been thinking about how his half-brother Jesus was treated. It wasn't the common people who dragged him into court, but those from the top echelons of society. And in many parts of the world those who hold power are still persecuting the poor. Often those who exploit the poor are the same ones who slander 'the noble name of him to whom you belong' (verse 7).

James wants us to remember that we bear the name of Christ: we are members of his kingdom, we belong to him, we love him. And all that is true of us is true of the believer who is poor.

Care for the poor isn't an isolated issue mentioned only in James's letter. It is a core theme that pulsates throughout Scripture. We are following God the Father and the example of Christ if we love the poor.

Spend time meditating on Isaiah 58:6–8:

> Is not this the kind of fasting I have chosen:
> to loose the chains of injustice
>   and untie the cords of the yoke,
> to set the oppressed free
>   and break every yoke?
> Is it not to share your food with the hungry
>   and to provide the poor wanderer with shelter –
> when you see the naked, to clothe them,
>   and not to turn away from your own flesh and
>   blood?
> Then your light will break forth like the dawn,
>   and your healing will quickly appear;
> then your righteousness will go before you,
>   and the glory of the Lord will be your rear guard.

Consider your own situation, opportunities and sphere of influence. How is God asking you to demonstrate love and care for the poor?

Day 10

Read James 2:5–13
Key verses: James 2:8–13

••

⁸If you really keep the royal law found in Scripture, 'Love your neighbour as yourself,' you are doing right. ⁹But if you show favouritism, you sin and are convicted by the law as law-breakers. ¹⁰For whoever keeps the whole law and yet stumbles at just one point is guilty of breaking all of it. ¹¹For he who said, 'You shall not commit adultery,' also said, 'You shall not murder.' If you do not commit adultery but do commit murder, you have become a law-breaker.

¹²Speak and act as those who are going to be judged by the law that gives freedom, ¹³because judgment without mercy will be shown to anyone who has not been merciful. Mercy triumphs over judgment.

We are sons and daughters of the King. This means we have privileges but also responsibilities.

We are subject to the royal law that tells us to love our neighbour as ourselves (verse 8). James reminds us that we are not free to be selective, but must apply this law across the board. Notice, he adds, that this law condemns those who break it, but liberates those who keep it.

So, for example, picture a poor person – someone in need, whom you're tempted to think is a nuisance and isn't going to help you at all. When you obey the law to love that person as yourself, it's remarkably liberating. It liberates you from many of your fears, prejudices and selfishness, and you begin to find yourself free to love and care. But if you don't, you will find that you are constrained by your own selfishness, greed and supercilious attitude, and you're condemned.

Having been trained as a bank manager, I find it the easiest thing in the world to evaluate people quickly, to be critical and dismiss them with alacrity. But I have discovered that if I am to be a member of the kingdom and see people as God sees them, evaluate them as God evaluates them and operate under the royal law of the King which requires me to love my neighbour as myself, then I will stop being critical, analytical and judgmental, and begin to be merciful, kind and generous towards them. And the remarkable thing is that I find myself wonderfully liberated. But every time I refuse, I find myself in a straitjacket of my own prejudice.

Most of us find it very easy to be critical of others. So the command to 'love your neighbour as yourself' is staggering:

> It seems to demand that I tear the skin off my body and wrap it around another person so that I feel that I am that other person; and all the longings that I have for my own safety and health and success and happiness I now feel for that other person as though he were me.
> (John Piper, www.desiringgod.org/messages/love-your-neighbor-as-yourself-part-1, 30 April 1995)

But notice that the second part of this royal law overflows from the first (Luke 10:27). Loving others is the natural consequence of wholeheartedly loving God. Invite the Holy Spirit to work in your heart today so that your love for God deepens, manifesting itself in loving others. No more criticism, snap judgments or snide comments. Let mercy triumph over judgment!

Day 11

Read James 2:14–19
Key verses: James 2:14–17

. . . .

> [14]*What good is it, my brothers and sisters, if someone claims to have faith but has no deeds? Can such faith save them?* [15]*Suppose a brother or a sister is without clothes and daily food.* [16]*If one of you says to them, 'Go in peace; keep warm and well fed,' but does nothing about their physical needs, what good is it?* [17]*In the same way, faith by itself, if it is not accompanied by action, is dead.*

These verses have courted a lot of controversy. Martin Luther, in particular, was concerned that James was teaching justification by works, in direct contrast to Paul's doctrine of justification by grace through faith.

But James's question in verse 14: 'Can such faith save them?' indicates that he assumes people can be saved and that they are saved by faith. However, his point is that some faith can be fake, and therefore needs to be carefully evaluated.

It is not just *what* we believe that is important; James wants to underline that *how* we believe is tremendously significant. The object of our faith determines the validity of our faith; you can put minimal faith in thick ice and be safe. Conversely, you can have great faith in thin ice and you will drown. Yes, what you put your faith in is of vital importance. But James is adamant that the calibre and quality of our faith are also desperately important.

The example James uses here is that faith is dead if it is devoid of compassion. Faith is demonstrated by our obedience to the Lord. The Lord has required us to adhere to the royal law. Therefore, if the royal law says I should love my neighbour, and I say, 'I have faith in the Lord of that law', then the reality of my faith will be shown in the compassion I demonstrate in obedience to that command.

If you were brought into a court of law, would there be enough evidence to convict you as a Christian? Would your neighbours, work colleagues, family members and friends say your faith was something you just talked about, or something that had a significant impact on your life?

Using James's example, when was the last time you showed compassion? Being compassionate can be exhausting and time-consuming. It means our own agenda is put on hold, as we get involved in other people's lives. Certainly there is little reward or glamour dealing with the practical, mundane matters of everyday life. But it is living proof of your faith. Look for heaven-sent opportunities to demonstrate compassion today.

Day 12

Read James 2:14–19
Key verses: James 2:18–19

....

¹⁸ *But someone will say, 'You have faith; I have deeds.'*
Show me your faith without deeds, and I will show
you my faith by my deeds. ¹⁹ *You believe that there is*
one God. Good! Even the demons believe that –
and shudder.

Should we use creeds in our worship services?

Creeds can be wonderful tools for learning and discovering the faith. But it is also possible to recite them in a way that is totally devoid of meaning and content.

'You believe that there is one God' (verse 19) probably relates to the great statement in Deuteronomy 6:4, the beginning of the Shema, which orthodox Jews would recite every single day: 'The LORD our God, the LORD is one.'

But there is no point in reciting a creed and thinking that makes us all right. Even the demons believe the creeds! 'The demons believe – and shudder' (verse 19). The demons believe thoroughly and are shaken by what they believe, but no-one imagines that the demons are saved!

There is no merit in saying, 'Well, I go in for faith, you go in for works. I'm a passive, contemplative sort and you are a doer.' We can't create these divisions. Indeed, James is adamant that this dichotomy doesn't exist – it is not either-or; it is both-and. Faith and deeds are not optional.

If we are a people of faith, we will be a people of action, looking for ways to demonstrate our faith. As James urges us repeatedly, 'Show me your faith.'

Some of us tend towards social action; others are keener to open the Bible with people. But the challenge, the glorious vision, is to hold both these aspects together and minister to the whole person.

• Think about the friendships you have with non-Christians. How can you demonstrate that you truly care? In what ways are you 'showing your faith' as well as talking about it?
• Think about the ways you serve in church – looking after the children in crèche, providing transportation

for the elderly and serving meals to international students, for example. What is your motivation, your reason for serving? What drives you to keep on going?

Pray today for opportunities to 'show your faith' in practical, God-honouring ways.

Day 13

Read James 2:14–26
Key verses: James 2:20–26

. . . .

[20] You foolish person, do you want evidence that faith without deeds is useless? [21] Was not our father Abraham considered righteous for what he did when he offered his son Isaac on the altar? [22] You see that his faith and his actions were working together, and his faith was made complete by what he did. [23] And the scripture was fulfilled that says, 'Abraham believed God, and it was credited to him as righteousness,' and he was called God's friend. [24] You see that a person is considered righteous by what they do and not by faith alone.

[25] In the same way, was not even Rahab the prostitute considered righteous for what she did when she gave lodging to the spies and sent them off in a different direction? [26] As the body without the spirit is dead, so faith without deeds is dead.

'Look at the evidence!'

This is James's challenge to us.

Perhaps he is responding to a person who challenged him during his sermon. Or possibly he is engaging in 'diatribe', an old Jewish way of communicating. Either way, we have an argument with someone here. James responds, 'Do you want evidence that faith without deeds is useless? Look at the life of Abraham.'

In verse 23 he quotes Genesis 15:6: 'Abraham believed God, and it was credited to him as righteousness.' How can we be sure that Abraham believed? Because of what he did. When God called him to go to a place and didn't tell him where it was, he went (Genesis 12). When God covenanted with him, he believed (Genesis 15). And the point James focuses on: when God told Abraham to sacrifice his son Isaac in whom all the covenant blessings were locked up, he was ready to obey (Genesis 22).

In complete contrast to the patriarch Abraham, James's second example is the disreputable Rahab. Hers was the oldest profession in the world. But when the children of Israel came to spy out Jericho, she told them she believed in their God: 'The LORD your God is God in heaven above and on the earth below' (Joshua 2:11). How do we know that she believed? She stuck her neck out! She rescued those men from certain death.

These two simple illustrations point to the fact that faith and actions go hand in hand. Just as the body without the Spirit is dead, so faith that doesn't demonstrate itself in compassion, concern, companionship and courage is not real faith at all. James is not saying that we are justified by these things – we are justified by grace through faith – but the evidence for saving faith is that it works. In the same way that a body without the Spirit is a corpse, so a faith that doesn't show itself in lively activities is dead.

It doesn't matter whether you come from a wealthy, respectable background like Abraham or have a chequered past like Rahab, you can be a friend of God (verse 23). This relationship is not dependent on your achievements, but solely on Christ's work on the cross. Of course, when you begin to understand all the implications of this new relationship, you experience a sense of gratitude, a desire to serve others and a passion to please God bubbling up inside. Living faith, by its very nature, produces righteous deeds. You may not feel as courageous as Abraham or Rahab, but today look for opportunities to put your faith into action. Is there something specific God is asking you to do? A promise you need to believe, a command you need to obey, a moral stand you need to take, a person you need to share the gospel with?

Day 14

Read James 3:1–5
Key verse: James 3:1

••

¹Not many of you should become teachers, my fellow believers, because you know that we who teach will be judged more strictly.

'Sticks and stones may break my bones, but words will never hurt me' is a playground chant. But it is not true! Words are incredibly powerful and have potential for good or evil.

In this letter, James has been at great pains to remind us that true faith demonstrates itself in behaviour. And here he points out that our behaviour is often demonstrated in how we use our tongues.

He has already introduced the topic of the tongue in 1:26: 'Those who consider themselves religious and yet do not keep a tight rein on their tongues deceive themselves, and their religion is worthless.' And here in chapter 3 James starts by impressing on leaders the need to control their tongues.

In his day a teacher was addressed as 'Rabbi', which literally meant 'My great one': perhaps a fitting title for someone who was 'entrusted with the mysteries God has revealed' (1 Corinthians 4:1). Teachers were charged with explaining God's truth to others. And such a responsibility inevitably brought with it a privileged and prestigious role in society.

Today, as in past generations, we are in danger of inviting people to teach in church who perhaps ought not to hold that position. And sometimes, perhaps, with motives that are less than honourable, we want to be teaching when we may not be guarding ourselves as we ought.

Remember, 'From everyone who has been given much, much will be demanded; and from the one who has been entrusted with much, much more will be asked' (Luke 12:48).

James's message is primarily to preachers and church leaders. And while you may not have this particular role, you still have influence on others. Your children, grandchildren, the young people at church, younger Christians in your home group or Alpha course are listening how you speak about the Lord and others. They are listening how you respond to personal suffering and division in the church and they are watching whether the words you say match up with your actions.

Who is listening to your words? Who are you influencing? Recognize the privileged position God has entrusted to you. Pray for those taking note of your life. Determine, in God's strength, that your words will not bring them harm or discouragement, but rather will help them press on in the faith.

Set a guard over my mouth, Lord;
    keep watch over the door of my lips.
(Psalm 141:3)

Day 15

Read James 3:1–6
Key verses: James 3:2–5

....

²We all stumble in many ways. Anyone who is never at fault in what they say is perfect, able to keep their whole body in check.

³When we put bits into the mouths of horses to make them obey us, we can turn the whole animal. ⁴Or take ships as an example. Although they are so large and are driven by strong winds, they are steered by a very small rudder wherever the pilot wants to go. ⁵Likewise, the tongue is a small part of the body, but it makes great boasts. Consider what a great forest is set on fire by a small spark.

How do you measure maturity? Do you look for wrinkles, impressive qualifications and achievements, or someone's practical 'know-how'?

James believes maturity is measured by what comes out of our mouths.

In verses 2–5 James, with characteristic skill, makes use of a variety of illustrations. He thinks of a horse with a bit in its mouth, a great ship out at sea, and a little spark setting off a raging forest fire. His point is that this little member of our body that so often we don't regard as particularly significant is in fact phenomenally important, because unless it is controlled, it leads to all kinds of disaster and damage. Conversely, this little member, if it is properly controlled, will lead to the control of one's whole life.

Consequently, the tongue is a measure of maturity. If someone's tongue is out of control, that person is invariably spiritually, emotionally or intellectually immature. If, on the other hand, someone speaks wisely, judiciously, carefully, positively and helpfully, you have found a mature individual.

And spiritual maturity is God's goal for us (Ephesians 4:13–15). As Paul explains,

> Not that I have already obtained all this, or have already arrived at my goal, but I press on to take hold of that for which Christ Jesus took hold of me . . . forgetting what is behind and straining towards what is ahead, I press on towards the goal to win the prize for which God has called me heavenwards in Christ Jesus.
> (Philippians 3:12–14)

Will you press on to maturity?

What does your language say about you?

What do the jokes you laugh at, the gossip you share, your comments about church leaders or employers reveal about you? How well do you fare on the maturity meter? Could God be asking you to 'grow up'?

It is very easy to say whatever pops into our heads, speak simply to fill the silence and destroy someone with an unkind word. It is much harder and requires more prayerful discipline to control our tongue. Meditate on the following verses as you press on to maturity:

May these words of my mouth and this meditation
    of my heart
  be pleasing in your sight,
  O Lord, my Rock and my Redeemer.
(Psalm 19:14)

Like apples of gold in settings of silver
  is a ruling rightly given.
(Proverbs 25:11)

Do not let any unwholesome talk come out of your mouths, but only what is helpful for building others up according to their needs, that it may benefit those who listen.
(Ephesians 4:29)

Day 16

Read James 3:1–12
Key verses: James 3:5–12

. . . .

⁵ *Likewise, the tongue is a small part of the body, but it makes great boasts. Consider what a great forest is set on fire by a small spark.* ⁶ *The tongue also is a fire, a world of evil among the parts of the body. It corrupts the whole body, sets the whole course of one's life on fire, and is itself set on fire by hell.*

⁷ *All kinds of animals, birds, reptiles and sea creatures are being tamed and have been tamed by mankind,* ⁸ *but no human being can tame the tongue. It is a restless evil, full of deadly poison.*

⁹ *With the tongue we praise our Lord and Father, and with it we curse human beings, who have been made in God's likeness.* ¹⁰ *Out of the same mouth come praise and cursing. My brothers and sisters, this should not be.* ¹¹ *Can both fresh water and salt water flow from the same spring?* ¹² *My brothers and sisters, can a fig-tree bear olives, or a grapevine bear figs? Neither can a salt spring produce fresh water.*

A hastily written email, a sharply worded text, an outburst of anger when we are tired can all cause immense damage.

Our words are so powerful because they reveal our true thoughts and attitudes. Our words, even careless ones, show what our hearts are like.

Using a series of illustrations, James forces us to dwell on this point. He describes our tongues as:

• a spark from hell

   That spark of godlessness, rebellion, and obscenity in our speech is set on fire in hell. Just like the forest fire, the damage is irreparable; it corrupts our whole body, producing a 'world of evil'.

• a wild animal

   Although we can train wild animals, it is a strange irony that we can't tame our tongues. When we don't bring them under control, they become a 'restless evil'.

• a polluted well

   It would be strange to go to a well and sometimes draw fresh water and at other times draw salt water. Similarly, it is inconsistent and unacceptable to use our tongue both to praise God *and* to hurt someone made in his image. How we treat one another is actually a marker of what we think of God.

• a fruit tree

You can tie apples onto a pear tree, but it does not make it an apple tree. The fruit of the tree demonstrates its root. Similarly, what comes out of my mouth is an indication of what is going on in my heart.

Your casual conversations, your responses when you are tired or angry, your comments about people when they are not present all reveal the state of your heart (Matthew 12:34–35). So guarding your tongue begins with guarding your heart (Proverbs 4:23). What measures are you taking to look after your heart? Are you taking double-pronged action – not only steering away from negative influences, but pursuing positive ones? Think about the programmes you watch, websites you browse, books you read and music you listen to. Ask the Holy Spirit to help you guard your heart today so that the words you say are wise, honest and helpful.

Day 17

Read James 3:13–16
Key verse: James 3:13

....

13Who is wise and understanding among you? Let them show it by their good life, by deeds done in the humility that comes from wisdom.

Are you living the good life?

Our society and media portray the good life in terms of acquiring 'goods' or possessions. We are living the good life if we can buy what we want when we want it, if we can indulge our every whim.

However, the word 'good' used by James in verse 13 means 'good' in the sense of 'lovely' – not superficially glamorous, but intrinsically beautiful; not extravagant, but significant.

God's good life is not found in acquiring possessions, but is the result of wisdom that is deeply embedded in the heart and demonstrates itself in our behaviour, and particularly in our speech.

Where can we find this sort of wisdom? Proverbs 9:10 tells us that 'The fear of the LORD is the beginning of wisdom.' In other words, it is only when we begin to understand who the Lord is, and what role he plays in our lives, that we're even close to the beginning of wisdom.

This wisdom that begins with acknowledging who the Lord is blossoms into 'understanding' (verse 13). The word 'understanding' means 'well-informed'. So the fear of the Lord begins to inform a person about all aspects of life. The Lord is integrated into all dimensions of his or her being. Sometimes we try to keep the Lord and spiritual things in a watertight compartment, separate and distinct from the rest of our life. But James insists that this wisdom that begins with the fear of the Lord permeates every dimension of our being and every aspect of our lives.

This is the good life.

To the world, the good life is about acquiring 'things'. The more 'things' we have, the more 'things' we can do, the better our life must be. In complete contrast, Jesus says that the good life is not pursuing *many* things, only *one* – him.

Perhaps you need to hear his words to Martha: 'You are worried and upset about many things, but few things are needed – or indeed only one' (Luke 10:41–42).

This single pursuit of Christ is liberating. You no longer need to be looking over your shoulder at what others have or what they are doing; you don't have to strive to impress anyone; your worth is not determined by your bank account. Instead, your sole aim, your glorious lifelong ambition, is to pursue Christ. So today, at regular points, perhaps on the hour, pause to worship God; look for every opportunity to obey him and uphold his values. Today, live for an audience of One.

Day 18

Read James 3:13–16
Key verse: James 3:13

• •

13Who is wise and understanding among you? Let them show it by their good life, by deeds done in the humility that comes from wisdom.

We have all met them.

Christians who walk into a room with an 'I've arrived, look at me' attitude; believers who radiate an 'I know it all' aura.

But this is worlds away from James's call to demonstrate our 'good life by deeds done in humility that comes from wisdom'. Godly wisdom is displayed not by a superior attitude, but by our humility. The word is 'meekness'. It is not the same as weakness. Rather, it is strength that chooses not to exert itself. Humility is not someone simply pretending to be terribly submissive and persuaded. Someone with humility has a genuine, realistic evaluation of self, and is prepared to respond and yield to what is going on.

In 1:21 James uses the word 'meekness' again, concerning our attitude to the Word of God. Calvin says that it means we have 'a mind disposed to learn' from the Scriptures. We are to have a humble attitude towards God and his Word.

When it comes to our relationship with God, we have an awful lot to be humble about. Therefore, humility and meekness would seem very appropriate indeed. Meekness towards the Word, towards God and towards people – that is heavenly wisdom.

If you've gotten anything at all out of following Christ, if his love has made any difference in your life, if being in a community of the Spirit means anything to you, if you have a heart, if you *care* – then do me a favour: Agree with each other, love each other, be deep-spirited friends. Don't push your way to the front; don't sweet-talk your way to the top. Put yourself aside, and help others get ahead. Don't be obsessed with getting your own advantage. Forget yourselves long enough to lend a helping hand.

Think of yourselves the way Christ Jesus thought of himself. He had equal status with God but didn't think so much of himself that he had to cling to the advantages of that status no matter what . . . Instead, he lived a selfless, obedient life and then died a selfless, obedient death – and the worst kind of death at that – a crucifixion.

(Philippians 2:1–8, MSG)

Don't be afraid to be counter-cultural. Follow Jesus' example and willingly humble yourself. Be humble in how you approach God, how you respond to his Word and how you treat other people. Then, just as God exalted Christ, one day he will exalt you. Humility now means glory later!

Day 19

Read James 3:14–18
Key verses: James 3:14–16

....

14 But if you harbour bitter envy and selfish ambition in your hearts, do not boast about it or deny the truth. 15 Such 'wisdom' does not come down from heaven but is earthly, unspiritual, demonic. 16 For where you have envy and selfish ambition, there you find disorder and every evil practice.

Sometimes our common sense and God's wisdom converge, but not always. Take care not to confuse the two.

James points out that there are two types of wisdom. There is a wisdom that comes from heaven (verse 17), but there is another kind of wisdom – 'earthly, unspiritual, demonic' – which has to be guarded against.

Much of earthly wisdom is sound common sense, but it is devoid of any spiritual understanding. So, for example, the Spirit of God may call you to share the gospel in a dangerous location, but your unbelieving family, being highly practical and very realistic, dissuade you, telling you it is a crazy thing to do. That is earthly wisdom and it is unspiritual. Yes, a good loving family can pump wisdom into us that is purely secular, has nothing to do with the Spirit and manages to achieve the devil's end.

It happened to Peter. He didn't want the Lord to go to Jerusalem, because he loved him and didn't want him to be in danger. Did Jesus turn on him and say, 'Thank you for that very sensible, solid advice'? No! He said, 'Get behind me, Satan!' (Mark 8:33). Sometimes totally common-sense arguments from well-meaning people will achieve purely secular, humanistic, devilish ends. That is why it is utterly imperative that we keep in step with the Spirit.

In verse 16 James points out that the wrong advice, being estranged from heavenly wisdom and out of touch with the Word of God and the Spirit of God, being out of step with divine purposes, can mean you become inordinately concerned about yourself (that's what envy means here), totally committed to looking out for number one, and pursuing your own dream of the good life.

God's plans often contradict common sense. For example:

- planting a church in your village instead of joining the more established fellowship in the next town;
- turning down a well-paid job in order to work for a Christian charity;
- encouraging your children to train and be involved in full-time Christian ministry rather than secular employment;
- giving generously to kingdom ministry rather than stockpiling for your pension or a rainy day.

Make sure you are not being swept along with the world's distorted view of the good life. Instead, make every effort to 'keep in step with the Spirit' (Galatians 5:22–26; see also Romans 8:9–14).

Trust in the LORD with all your heart
    and lean not on your own understanding;
in all your ways submit to him,
    and he will make your paths straight.
Do not be wise in your own eyes;
    fear the LORD and shun evil.
(Proverbs 3:5–7)

Day 20

Read James 3:13–18
Key verses: James 3:17–18

• •

17 But the wisdom that comes from heaven is first of all pure; then peace-loving, considerate, submissive, full of mercy and good fruit, impartial and sincere. 18 Peacemakers who sow in peace reap a harvest of righteousness.

What is the hallmark of this 'wisdom that comes from heaven'? How can you tell if someone is wise, according to God's definition?

Using his favourite phrase, 'show me' (verse 13; see also 2:18), James has already underlined that wisdom needs to be visible and tangible. So what is the evidence?

You can tell the people who are deriving wisdom from above, who are integrating it into their lives so that it is becoming the dominant factor in their thinking about life, because they become increasingly:

- *pure* – related to the word 'holy' and meaning free from blemish;

- *peace-loving* and peace-making (James himself exemplified this in Acts 15 and 21);

- *considerate* – accepting, amenable and not inflexible;

- *submissive* – being persuasive in communication and capable of being persuaded;

- *merciful* – having a concern and reaching out practically to those who are hurting;

- *impartial* – not in two minds;

- *sincere* – the word is often translated 'not hypocritical'. The Greek word for hypocrite is a 'play actor'. Actors in those days hid behind a mask, and their own feelings were irrelevant. A hypocrite is someone who lives behind a mask.

How are these virtues demonstrated? There is going to be a 'sowing in peace'. St Augustine actually defined peace as 'the tranquillity of order'. Those who are living out God's wisdom are people of peace, whose lives are in order and are concerned about bringing order. There is also a great concern for putting things right. Such wisdom results in a 'harvest of righteousness', which means right living, right behaviour, treating people right and living rightly before God.

What a crop! What a harvest!

How wise are you? To what extent have you grown in wisdom this past week, month or year?

Growth in wisdom is measurable – not in increased possessions, university degrees or even the number of candles on your birthday cake, but in the increase in these godly virtues, in your growth in godliness.

Pray that God's wisdom would be integrated more and more into your life and increasingly on display in your:

- marriage
- family life
- credit card statement
- attitude to work/career/unemployment/retirement
- worship
- Bible reading
- contribution to church life.

Imagine what an advertisement we would be for Christ if every day we were pure, peace-loving, considerate, submissive, merciful, impartial and sincere . . .

Imagine how different our conversations and behaviour would be if our driving passion were to live righteously before God . . .

Imagine the impact on our family, workplace or street if God's wisdom dictated every area of our life . . .

Imagine how different our church would be if careless conversations were replaced with a concern to treat people right and to put situations right . . .

Imagine . . .

Day 21

Read James 4:1–3
Key verse: James 4:1

....

¹What causes fights and quarrels among you? Don't they come from your desires that battle within you?

Stop burying your head in the sand! Don't ignore the tensions any longer. Ask yourself the hard question James poses here.

Although he has been talking about God's wisdom producing a peace-loving, peace-making lifestyle, as far as this very practical man is concerned we have to face up to the fact that war, strife, tension, violence, disintegration and disorderliness are everywhere. As well as international and national conflict, we have family breakdown, marital discord and even schisms within our church fellowships.

James himself doesn't shy away from answering his own question: 'What causes fights and quarrels among you?

Don't they come from your desires that battle within you?'

He has talked about 'desires' before (1:14–15), and has been careful to point out that the perfectly legitimate desires God has planted within us can become warped and twisted and agents of devilish activity. He not only talks about 'desires', but also in verse 2 he speaks of 'wants' and 'coveting'.

This belief that one owes it to oneself to experience everything that gives pleasure is called hedonism. This is the dominating ethos of our generation and inevitably leads to the disintegration of society. Of course it does! If I am only interested in myself, I am going to become so utterly dominated by my intrinsic self-ism and become so selfish that I will have no time for anyone else. And when others' self-interest collides with mine, there will be squabbles and fights.

At the root of the fights we see internationally, nationally, in families, marriages and churches is what Freud called the 'pleasure principle': these desires, wants and covet-ousness are the evidence of self-centredness. Alec Motyer says, 'It is at root no more than the existence in each of us of a self-centred heart, a controlling spirit of self-interest' (*The Message of James*, IVP, 1998, p. 145).

How sobering to think that the squabbles in my church, marriage and family boil down to this 'pleasure principle'. It may seem that they hang on other issues, such as style of worship or which side of the family to spend Christmas day with. But James is saying that, in essence, the problem is that I am selfish and want my own way.

If you are involved in any sort of quarrel, ask God to search your heart and show you where the selfishness lies. Ask him to give you the strength to put 'self' to death and put the needs of others first.

Meditate on what Jesus' words mean for you in your own particular situation: 'Whoever wants to be my disciple must deny themselves and take up their cross daily and follow me' (Luke 9:23).

Day 22

Read James 4:1–3
Key verses: James 4:2–3

....

²You desire but do not have, so you kill. You covet but you cannot get what you want, so you quarrel and fight. You do not have because you do not ask God. ³When you ask, you do not receive, because you ask with wrong motives, that you may spend what you get on your pleasures.

How would you describe your church prayer meeting? Vibrant? Small? Stagnant? Perhaps you have never attended.

Interestingly, the second reason James gives for the tensions and fights Christians experience is to do with prayer. He raises two issues:

• Prayerlessness

'You do not have because you do not ask God' (verse 2). It is fairly easy for believers to live their church life purely on the basis of self-effort, self-assertion and self-interest. You don't need to pray to operate on any, or all, of these principles. Does your church operate on these principles? Or is there a higher, nobler objective – to begin to discover what the will of God is, to identify with the plan of God, to live in the power of God and produce a church that is explicable only in terms of divine intervention in human affairs?

- Inappropriate prayer

  'When you ask, you do not receive, because you ask with wrong motives, that you may spend what you get on your pleasures' (verse 3). Sometimes our prayers end with that lovely little phrase, 'for Jesus' sake', but they have nothing to do with Jesus' sake; it's for *our* sake. We might try to legitimize our prayers by adding 'for Jesus' sake', but we are not really concerned about the honour of Christ, the extension of his kingdom, the hallowing of his name or doing his will on earth as it is done in heaven. What we are really concerned with is self-interest.

What difference would it make in your church if nobody prayed? Sometimes we get so caught up in our own efforts and agenda that we actually forget to pray. And so we miss out on seeing God at work. Instead of God's power and glory being showcased, arguments and tensions fester.

Prayer is our opportunity to enter God's throne room – to enjoy his presence, experience his peace, recognize our dependence on him, learn his will and join him in his work.

What are you praying for now? How different would your prayer requests be if you really prayed 'for Jesus' sake'?

Day 23

Read James 4:1–5
Key verses: James 4:4–5

....

> ⁴*You adulterous people, don't you know that friend-ship with the world means enmity against God? Therefore, anyone who chooses to be a friend of the world becomes an enemy of God.* ⁵*Or do you think Scripture says without reason that he jealously longs for the spirit he has caused to dwell in us?*

James does not pull any punches. He is relentless in his efforts to help us understand how conflicts and tensions arise among us.

The term 'adulterous' here does not necessarily mean that James's readers are engaging in sexual immorality. He is simply using an Old Testament illustration (Hosea 1:2). In effect, he's saying that God's people sometimes claim to be betrothed to Christ, but have actually gone off with other lovers. They've got their priorities wrong.

Instead of pursuing a friendship with God, they have chosen a friendship with the world.

What does it mean to have a friendship with the world? Definitions of 'worldliness' vary from place to place and age to age. But the Bible is actually quite explicit on what constitutes worldliness: it is 'the lust of the flesh, the lust of the eyes, and the pride of life' (1 John 2:16).

So when we think in terms of worldliness, we have to decide: is God my friend, or is my desire for position (the pride of life), possessions and passions (the lust of the flesh and the lust of the eyes) the dominating factor? If those are my chief concerns, and if everyone in the fellowship is like that, everything will be wonderful! Until your passions and my passions collide, or your position challenges my position, or your possessions are better than my possessions. Then all kinds of tensions will result (verse 1).

There has to be something grander than this, and there is. It's the love of God.

So what is the priority? Which path will you choose?

There is an antagonism between God and the world; there's a mutually exclusive friendship and enmity. It is either-or. Either we are motivated by the Spirit, or we are motivated by intrinsic selfishness.

When you put it as starkly as this – friendship with God or friendship with the world – it hardly seems much of a choice. But usually the temptations of position, possessions and passions creep upon us stealthily and are altogether more subtle. Pinpoint your weaknesses regarding friendship with the world. Where will the devil most likely pounce: the lusts of the flesh, the lusts of the eyes or the pride of life? With God's help, keep on your guard. Pray also for members of your family and church – those in your small group, those you serve on a rota with, your prayer partner – that they too would choose friendship with God today.

Finally, be strong in the Lord and in his mighty power. Put on the full armour of God, so that you can take your stand against the devil's schemes. For our struggle is not against flesh and blood, but against the rulers, against the authorities, against the powers of this dark world and against the spiritual forces of evil in the heavenly realms.

(Ephesians 6:10–12)

Day 24

Read James 4:1–6
Key verse: James 4:6

....

⁶But he gives us more grace. That is why Scripture says:

'God opposes the proud
but shows favour to the humble.'

Have you been following James' argument so far?

He's saying, 'If you want to show me your faith, show me your works.' One of the works we can anticipate is that you'll be a peace-loving, peaceable, peace-making person. But we do this in the midst of various tensions and conflicts.

James has given a number of reasons for these struggles: our selfishness, our prayerlessness and wrong motives in prayer, our pursuit of worldliness rather than Christ. The final reason he identifies here is pride.

Quoting Proverbs 3:34, James sets out the two options. On the one hand, if I insist on exalting myself in the fellowship of believers, there are others who will accept it as their God-given responsibility to bring me down. If you have a church with a lot of proud, arrogant people who are becoming increasingly hard and embittered and committed to their own way of doing things, it's only a matter of time until you have all kinds of problems.

On the other hand, if I insist on humbling myself before God and laying myself low before him, I'm in the right position – I am waiting for God's grace and favour; I am waiting for him to raise me up. You see, my worth doesn't depend on the adulation of others; it is only God's exaltation that counts. I can humble myself before others, I can be open and honest with them, and I can trust God with my reputation and all the circumstances of my life, because he has promised to raise me up one day.

Reflect honestly: is there any evidence of pride in your life? Signs could be: always assuming you are right; reluctance to ask for advice; satisfaction in one's own achievements; or a determination to protect one's reputation.

In the final analysis we have little to be proud about. All we are and have comes from Christ, and any self-aggrandizement will pale into insignificance compared to the way God will exalt us.

Be willing to humble yourself, and wait for God to exalt you. Join the frequent refrain of Scripture: 'Let the one who boasts boast in the Lord' (1 Corinthians 1:31; see also Psalms 34:2; 44:8; 2 Corinthians 10:17).

This is what the LORD says:
'Let not the wise boast of their wisdom
    or the strong boast of their strength
    or the rich boast of their riches,
but let the one who boasts boast about this:
    that they have the understanding to know me,
that I am the LORD, who exercises kindness,
    justice and righteousness on earth,
    for in these I delight,'

                    declares the LORD.

(Jeremiah 9:23–24)

Consider what it means for you to 'boast in the Lord' and how you can do this today.

Day 25

Read James 4:5–12
Key verses: James 4:7–10

....

> [7] *Submit yourselves, then, to God. Resist the devil, and he will flee from you.* [8] *Come near to God and he will come near to you. Wash your hands, you sinners, and purify your hearts, you double-minded.* [9] *Grieve, mourn and wail. Change your laughter to mourning and your joy to gloom.* [10] *Humble yourselves before the Lord, and he will lift you up.*

How do we begin to address the problems in our hearts that so often engender strife in our marriages, families and churches?

By holding on to two spiritual truths.

First, recognize that God supplies grace to equip us to deal with the problem (verse 6). You can surely count on grace to deal with all that is required of you. Second, there are commands God gives which we must obey. In verses 7–10 we encounter some of the fifty-plus commands to be found in the 108 verses in James's letter.

Have you noticed how our temperament largely determines which of these spiritual truths we latch on to?

On the one hand, there are very detailed, organized, goal-setting individuals, who love immediate, measurable goals. These are the kind of people who make lists of the fifty-plus commands in James. They get out their stopwatches and computers, and they say, 'I've got twenty-four hours in a day and there are fifty commands here; fifty into twenty-four . . . Where's my clipboard? Tick, tick, tick.' If you are one of those people, remember there is grace available.

On the other hand, there are those who know grace is available, and they haven't even bothered to read the commands! They are just trusting God in his grace to do it. If this is your inclination, remember that these commands of God are to be taken seriously.

There is always a balance to be found. The old hymn puts it perfectly: 'Trust and obey.' We don't have to choose between appropriating God's grace and obeying his commands. Whichever comes naturally to you, ignore it, and concentrate on the other one!

If there are problems in your marriage, family or church, humble yourself before God. Analyse the situation before him, and on the basis of this, seek the grace of God to empower you to begin to rectify the problem, and then start being meticulously obedient.

If you do so, you will begin to demonstrate the reality of your faith.

Reread the commands listed in verses 7–10. Is there a particular command God is asking you to obey? In what way do you need to appropriate his grace? Pray through your day – the activities, concerns, people and situations you will have to deal with. Consider all the ways you will be able to demonstrate – to believers and unbelievers – the reality of your faith; all the ways your life can point them to God. Ask God to teach you what it means to both 'trust and obey' him in this season of your life.

Day 26

Read James 4:7–17
Key verses: James 4:13–17

....

[13] *Now listen, you who say, 'Today or tomorrow we will go to this or that city, spend a year there, carry on business and make money.' [14]Why, you do not even know what will happen tomorrow. What is your life? You are a mist that appears for a little while and then vanishes. [15]Instead, you ought to say, 'If it is the Lord's will, we will live and do this or that.' [16]As it is, you boast in your arrogant schemes. All such boasting is evil. [17]If anyone, then, knows the good they ought to do and doesn't do it, it is sin for them.*

At the end of personal letters, along with the signature, you used to see the initials DV. This was shorthand for *Deo volente* – God willing.

Nowadays, in the church as well as the world, attitudes have changed. We make plans with very little thought of God. In effect, we are saying, 'I've all the time in the world. I can go anywhere I wish. I can do my own thing. I will carry on business, and I'll make money.'

This attitude overlooks the simple fact that we don't even know what will happen tomorrow; we are like 'a mist that appears for a little while and then vanishes'. It is hard to see how anybody could be dominated by self-interest and self-assertion when Scripture says, 'You're like a mist'!

Instead of this arrogant, self-sufficient, self-assertive, self-interested lifestyle, which is the antithesis of a humble dependence on God and obedience to his commands, we ought to be saying, 'If this is the Lord's will, we will live and do this or that' (verse 15).

And if you persist in arrogance and refuse to humble yourself, you're not just creating all kinds of division and tension in your marriage, family and church; to put it bluntly, you're sinning. Because if you know the way to go, and you won't do it, that's rebellion.

We avoid thinking of ourselves as 'a mist', and we act and plan as if we will be around for ever. We may seek God's will for the big decisions – who to marry and where to live – but we tend not to consult him on the smaller, daily decisions because we feel able to handle these on our own. How foolish!

Recognize that what happens next, even your very breath, is DV – 'God willing'. All the plans you made for today are subject to his sovereignty. Don't let arrogance and self-confidence lead you into sin and rebellion. Humbly submit your plans to him. Pray that instead of holding on tightly to your own agenda, you will be obedient to all that God wants you to do today.

> In their hearts humans plan their course,
>> but the LORD establishes their steps.
>
> (Proverbs 16:9)

Day 27

Read James 5:1–20
Key verses: James 5:1–6

....

¹Now listen, you rich people, weep and wail because of the misery that is coming on you. ²Your wealth has rotted, and moths have eaten your clothes. ³Your gold and silver are corroded. Their corrosion will testify against you and eat your flesh like fire. You have hoarded wealth in the last days. ⁴Look! The wages you failed to pay the workers who mowed your fields are crying out against you. The cries of the harvesters have reached the ears of the Lord Almighty. ⁵You have lived on earth in luxury and self-indulgence. You have fattened yourselves in the day of slaughter. ⁶You have condemned and murdered the innocent one, who was not opposing you.

While major segments of the world are dying because of malnutrition, in the West people are dying because of their extravagant indulgence.

James now turns to address these sins of prosperity. Having talked about humility, speech, silly squabbles in church, messy marriages and bad relationships, James now speaks about money. It shouldn't be surprising that faith is demonstrated not only in our conversations and relationships, but also in our bank statements and direct debits.

Verses 1–6 are James's diatribe against prosperity. It is not sinful to be wealthy. God owns the cattle on a thousand hills; Abraham was very wealthy; Jacob became wealthy; Jesus was buried in the tomb of a wealthy man. So prosperity in and of itself is not sinful.

But there are issues we must consider:

- The means that we use to gain prosperity may be sinful.

- The attitudes that prosperity produces may well be sinful.

- The way we utilize our prosperity may be sinful.

In these verses, James is talking about extravagance, indulgence, selfishness – all the sins that come through prosperity. He's asking us to look at what we have and how we could better reflect our faith in God.

Whether we have a little or a lot, we tend to become attached to our money. Think through James's points: how do you gain your money, what is your attitude to it and how do you spend it? As a practical exercise, look through your bank statement: what are you spending most of your money on? What amount are you giving back to God? Is there evidence of indulgence or greed? Be willing for the Holy Spirit to point out some painful home truths. As you make your next purchase, pay your next bill, receive your next pay cheque, pray that God would fix in your mind a godly view of resources: we are stewards of his money and will one day be called to give an account.

Day 28

Read James 5:1–20
Key verses: James 5:7–9

....

> [7] *Be patient, then, brothers and sisters, until the Lord's coming. See how the farmer waits for the land to yield its valuable crop, patiently waiting for the autumn and spring rains.* [8] *You too, be patient and stand firm, because the Lord's coming is near.* [9] *Don't grumble against one another, brothers and sisters, or you will be judged. The Judge is standing at the door!*

The Lord is coming again.

Christians have an end in view. We know history is not just repeating itself meaninglessly, nor is it a chance collision of circumstances. It is the unfolding of the divine purpose, and God is working inevitably, relentlessly, inexorably towards the consummation of his eternal will.

Part of God's will is that at the appropriate time, Christ will return. James reminds us about this future hope (verses

7–9) because it needs to inform how we live now. Knowing that Christ will return and we will live with him for ever is a powerful motivator to holy living: to put our faith into action in our speech, relationships at home and church, our plans, how we use our money – and all the other examples James has given in his letter.

James is echoing the apostle Peter's plea:

> Therefore, with minds that are alert and fully sober, set your hope on the grace to be brought to you when Jesus Christ is revealed at his coming. As obedient children, do not conform to the evil desires you had when you lived in ignorance. But just as he who called you is holy, so be holy in all you do; for it is written: 'Be holy, because I am holy.'
> (1 Peter 1:13–15)

> Since everything will be destroyed in this way, what kind of people ought you to be? You ought to live holy and godly lives as you look forward to the day of God and speed its coming. That day will bring about the destruction of the heavens by fire, and the elements will melt in the heat. But in keeping with his promise we are looking forward to a new heaven and a new earth, where righteousness dwells.
> (2 Peter 3:11–13)

'The Lord is coming again': whisper it to yourself, repeat it aloud and let the truth and magnitude of these words sink into your soul afresh. He could return this morning or before you get home from work tonight. Keep this glorious thought in the forefront of your mind today. Let it shape how you speak to your children and spouse, apply yourself to your work, use your free time, deal with church conflict and decide what to purchase.

With all that lies ahead and all we have to look forward to, use this waiting time to grow in godliness and prepare yourself for your new home 'where righteousness dwells'.

Day 29

Read James 5:1–20

Key verses: James 5:13–16

. . . .

¹³Is anyone among you in trouble? Let them pray. Is anyone happy? Let them sing songs of praise. ¹⁴Is anyone among you ill? Let them call the elders of the church to pray over them and anoint them with oil in the name of the Lord. ¹⁵And the prayer offered in faith will make the sick person well; the Lord will raise them up. If they have sinned, they will be forgiven. ¹⁶Therefore confess your sins to each other and pray for each other so that you may be healed. The prayer of a righteous person is powerful and effective.

There is nothing special about a well-known preacher's prayers, your pastor's prayers or your parents' prayers. Yes, it is good to have other people pray for you, but remember that you have direct access to God too.

Who does James exhort to pray? Those who are in trouble, happy or sick. That covers all of us, all of the time! Prayer is a powerful, dynamic force that makes a difference (verse 16).

In verse 14, James goes on to talk specifically about prayer for those who are sick. Notice we have the twin truths of obedience and faith mentioned again (see Day 25). There are commands to be obeyed: 'Let them pray. Let them sing songs of praise. Call for the elders.' But notice that when the elders are called to pray over someone who is sick, it is the prayer offered in faith that makes the sick person well. Both obedience and faith are required.

Does praying in faith always work? There have been many occasions when I, along with fellow elders in our church, have gone in faith and prayed over the sick. We have asked God to work, we have sought his face and God has always raised people up. Always.

That doesn't mean that they have been physically healed every time; they haven't. But everyone has testified to a tremendous spiritual uplift; everyone has testified to an emotional release; and not a few have testified to the fact that God has wonderfully healed them physically.

But remember: everyone who is healed subsequently goes to glory. So keep it in perspective!

Your prayers are precious to God; he listens and remembers each one.

> The four living creatures and the twenty-four elders fell down before the Lamb. Each one had a harp and they were holding golden bowls full of incense, which are the prayers of God's people.
> (Revelation 5:8)

Be obedient to God's commands and keep praying in faith, trusting him to act according to his will and in his time. Also, intercede for the believers whom God brings to your mind today. Ask him to 'raise' them up.

Day 30

Read James 5:1–20
Key verses: James 5:19–20

....

19 My brothers and sisters, if one of you should wander from the truth and someone should bring that person back, 20 remember this: whoever turns a sinner from the error of their way will save them from death and cover over a multitude of sins.

God loves wanderers (Matthew 9:36; Luke 15:4–7).

Indeed, Jesus left heaven when we were wandering to bring us back to God.

And now God invites us to join him in his mission and show our faith is working by bringing the wanderers home.

Of course, God is the One who ultimately brings wanderers home, but he does have a habit of using people in the process. So watch out for believers who wander from the truth, who start heaping up a multitude of sins because they are living in error. Don't hesitate to take action, because they are in danger of losing their souls.

If you turn wanderers back to God, you are engaged in the most wonderful work, which glorifies God, brings blessings and shows that your faith is working. You are being used to turn a sinner from error, to save a soul from death and to cover a multitude of sins.

None of us is immune to wanderlust. Each generation faces its own temptations, its own array of idols and attractive false teaching. Are you being intentional about spiritual growth and obedience to Christ? If not, it is easy to drift away from a God-focused life and be lured by the bright lights of the 'broad road' (Matthew 7:13).

Cling to Christ today. Don't let your heart be distracted by anything less.

> O to grace how great a debtor
> Daily I'm constrained to be!
> Let Thy goodness, like a fetter,
> Bind my wandering heart to Thee.
> Prone to wander, Lord, I feel it,
> Prone to leave the God I love;
> Here's my heart, O take and seal it,
> Seal it for Thy courts above.
> (Robert Robinson, 'Come, Thou Fount of Every Blessing',
> 1757)

Also, look out for your Christian friends and the others in your small group. Help them not to deviate from God's path: pray for one another, share deeply, speak out when you see sin, show heartfelt compassion, accept rebuke as from God and cheer each other on as you see the finish line ahead, so that each of you could say,

> I have fought the good fight, I have finished the race, I have kept the faith. Now there is in store for me the crown of righteousness, which the Lord, the righteous Judge, will award to me on that day – and not only to me, but also to all who have longed for his appearing. (2 Timothy 4:7–8)

For further study

If you would like to do further study on James's letter, the following books may be useful:

- Sam Allberry, *James for You* (The Good Book Company, 2015).

- R. Kent Hughes, *James: Faith that Works*, Preaching the Word (Crossway, 2015).

- Douglas Moo, *James*, Tyndale New Testament Commentaries (IVP, 2015).

- Alec Motyer, *The Message of James*, The Bible Speaks Today (IVP, 2014).

James mentions suffering a number of times in his short letter. If you would like to explore this subject further, there are many excellent resources available, including:

- Don Carson, *How Long, O Lord? Reflections on Suffering and Evil* (IVP, 2006).

- Sharon Dirckx, *Why? Looking at God, Evil and Personal Suffering* (IVP, 2013).

- Timothy Keller, *Walking with God through Pain and Suffering* (Hodder & Stoughton, 2015).
- Paul Mallard, *Invest Your Suffering: Unexpected Intimacy with a Loving God* (IVP, 2013).

KESWICK MINISTRIES

Our purpose

Keswick Ministries is committed to the spiritual renewal of God's people for his mission in the world.

God's purpose is to bring his blessing to all the nations of the world. That promise of blessing, which touches every aspect of human life, is ultimately fulfilled through the life, death, resurrection, ascension and future return of Christ. All of the people of God are called to participate in his missionary purposes, wherever he may place them. The central vision of *Keswick Ministries* is to see the people of God equipped, encouraged and refreshed to fulfil that calling, directed and guided by God's Word in the power of his Spirit, for the glory of his Son.

Our priorities

Keswick Ministries seeks to serve the local church through:

• *Hearing God's Word*: the Scriptures are the foundation for the church's life, growth and mission, and *Keswick Ministries* is committed to preach and teach God's Word in a way that is faithful to Scripture and relevant to Christians of all ages and backgrounds.

- *Becoming like God's Son*: from its earliest days the Keswick movement has encouraged Christians to live godly lives in the power of the Spirit, to grow in Christlikeness and to live under his lordship in every area of life. This is God's will for his people in every culture and generation.

- *Serving God's mission*: the authentic response to God's Word is obedience to his mission, and the inevitable result of Christlikeness is sacrificial service. *Keswick Ministries* seeks to encourage committed discipleship in family life, work and society, and energetic engagement in the cause of world mission.

Our ministry

- *Keswick: the event.* Every summer the town of Keswick hosts a three-week Convention, which attracts some 15,000 Christians from the UK and around the world. The event provides Bible teaching for all ages, vibrant worship, a sense of unity across generations and denominations, and an inspirational call to serve Christ in the world. It caters for children of all ages and has a strong youth and young adult programme. And it all takes place in the beautiful Lake District – a perfect setting for rest, recreation and refreshment.

- *Keswick: the movement.* For 140 years the work of Keswick has impacted churches worldwide, and today the movement is underway throughout the UK, as well as in many parts of Europe, Asia, North America, Australia, Africa and the Caribbean. *Keswick Ministries* is committed to strengthen the network in the UK and beyond, through prayer, news, pioneering and cooperative activity.

- *Keswick resources.* *Keswick Ministries* produces a range of books and booklets based on the core foundations of Christian life and mission. It makes Bible teaching available through free access to mp3 downloads, and the sale of DVDs and CDs. It broadcasts online through Clayton TV and annual BBC Radio 4 services.

- *Keswick teaching and training.* In addition to the summer Convention, Keswick Ministries is developing teaching and training events that will happen at other times of the year and in other places.

Our unity

The Keswick movement worldwide has adopted a key Pauline statement to describe its gospel inclusivity: 'for you are all one in Christ Jesus' (Galatians 3:28). *Keswick Ministries* works with evangelicals from a wide variety of church backgrounds, on the understanding that they share a commitment to the essential truths of the Christian faith as set out in our statement of belief.

Our contact details
T: 01768 780075
E: info@keswickministries.org
W: www.keswickministries.org
Mail: Keswick Ministries, Convention Centre, Skiddaw Street, Keswick CA12 4BY, England

related titles from IVP

FROM THE FOOD FOR THE JOURNEY SERIES

John 14 – 17
Simon Manchester
with Elizabeth McQuoid

ISBN: 978–1–78359–495–5
112 pages, paperback

The Food for the Journey series offers daily devotionals from much-loved Bible teachers at the Keswick Convention in an ideal pocket format – to accompany you wherever you go.

'This devotional by Simon Manchester, based on Jesus' final hours with his disciples, presents a series of sensitive and thought-provoking reflections that will challenge us as Christians to re-examine our responses to Christ's call to discipleship today.' Ivor Poobalan, Principal, Colombo Theological Seminary, Sri Lanka

'These devotional guides are excellent tools to enable us to hear God's Word in our day-to-day lives.' John Risbridger, Chair of Keswick Ministries, and Minister and Team Leader, Above Bar Church, Southampton

Also available

2 Timothy
Michael Baughen with Elizabeth McQuoid
1 Thessalonians
Alec Motyer with Elizabeth McQuoid
James
Stuart Briscoe with Elizabeth McQuoid